WOMEN
CIVIL WAR SPIES
OF THE UNION

LOIS SAKANY

The Rosen Publishing Group, Inc., New York

To my son, Isaiah

Published in 2004 by The Rosen Publishing Group, Inc.
29 East 21st Street, New York, NY 10010

Library of Congress Cataloging-in-Publication Data

Sakany, Lois.
Women Civil War spies of the Union/Lois Sakany.—1st ed.
    p. cm.—(American women at war)
Summary: Details the lives of six women who fought to preserve the
Union and to support abolition and women's rights by serving as spies
during the Civil War. Includes bibliographical references and index.
ISBN 0-8239-4450-6 (lib. bdg.)
1. Women spies—United States—Biography—Juvenile literature.
2. United States—History—Civil War, 1861–1865—Secret service—
Juvenile literature. 3. United States—History—Civil War,
1861–1865—Participation, Female—Juvenile literature. 4. United
States—History—Civil War, 1861–1865—Biography—Juvenile
literature. [1. Spies. 2. Women—Biography. 3. United States—History—
Civil War, 1861–1865—Secret service. 4. United States—History—Civil
War, 1861–1865—Participation, Female.]
I. Title. II. Series.
E608.S34 2004
973.7'85'0922—dc22

                                                           2003016698

Manufactured in the United States of America

On the front cover: This illustration shows Sarah Emma Edmonds,
a Union spy and war nurse, riding away from hospital tents toward a
battlefield.
On the back cover: An American flag

Contents

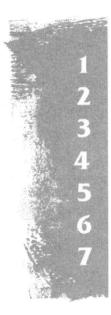

INTRODUCTION

The Civil War officially began in April 1861. However, the groundwork for one of the most important wars in U.S. history was set many years before. Even before the American Revolution, battle lines were being drawn between the North and the South over the issue of slavery.

As far back as 1787, state delegates at the Constitutional Convention in Philadelphia debated whether Congress should halt the importation of slaves. Delegates from South Carolina and

Georgia, whose economies depended on slave labor, threatened that their states would not join the planned Union if such a law were passed.

In the years before the start of the Civil War, talk of secession among the South's political leaders was common. When Abraham Lincoln, who ran on a platform of abolitionism and maintaining the Union, was elected into office as the United

This photograph of African men, women, and children was taken on a plantation around 1862 or 1863. By 1825, 36 percent of the world's slave population lived in the southern United States.

This 1861 print is entitled *Bombs at Fort Sumter.* Fort Sumter was named after a South Carolina Revolutionary War hero and was constructed in 1829. On April 12, 1861, Confederate brigadier general Beauregard attacked the Union garrison of Fort Sumter, beginning the U.S. Civil War. The Union forces were defeated and surrendered.

States's sixteenth president, all hope of holding the Union together was lost. On December 20, 1860, South Carolina seceded from the Union. Several other states quickly followed. Just before dawn, on April 12, 1861, the Confederate army fired on Fort Sumter in South Carolina and thus began the Civil War.

Prior to and during the Civil War, women were not permitted to vote, much less hold political office or assume positions in the military. Many women felt that they could do little more than support the decisions of their husbands and fathers. However, some women were not content to accept passive roles during such a turbulent time.

Before and during the war, many women used whatever means possible to make their voices heard. The feminist movement also gained steam during this period, and many of its leaders used the power of the written word to speak out against the inequalities that existed between men and women. For these women, taking up the cause of abolitionism was a natural extension of the fight for women's rights.

Ignoring the dictates of how "proper" women should behave, some women boldly chose to enter the fray of active service as undercover agents.

A photograph of Kady Brownell holding a sword. Brownell served in the Union army beside her husband and fought with the First Rhode Island Detached Militia and the Fifth Rhode Island Battalion. This picture postcard of the Civil War period was entitled *Daughter of the Regiment.*

Some of these women were ordinary citizens, while others were nurses or soldiers who disguised themselves as men and acted as spies whenever the opportunity arose.

Many of their stories remain untold. For the handful whose exploits were recorded, it is clear that they were nothing short of extraordinary. These women were not only unafraid to risk their own lives for the cause, but they also thought little of breaking out of the confines of a woman's place in their society. The backgrounds and experiences of female spies in the Civil War varied, but the trail the women blazed left a lasting impression.

SARAH E. THOMPSON

Civil War spy Sarah E. Thompson was born in Tennessee, a state that declared its allegiance to the rebel cause when it seceded in 1861. However, even after the state officially left the Union, many of its residents remained loyal to the Union, including Thompson. In addition to her covert activities, Thompson organized recruitment efforts, delivered dispatches, and served as a federal nurse. However, Thompson is best known for avenging her husband's death by bringing down Confederate general John Hunt Morgan.

Sarah Thompson, whose maiden name was Lane, was born in Green County, Tennessee, on February 11, 1838, twenty-three years before the start of the Civil War. When she was sixteen, she married Sylvanius H. Thompson, and they had two daughters. As a family, the Thompsons remained loyal to the Union cause.

Not long after the war began, Thompson's husband became a private in the First Tennessee Calvary U.S.A. By then, Tennessee had already seceded from the Union, and Sylvanius had to travel several days to Barberville, Kentucky, in order to sign on with the Union army. He was enrolled on July 12, 1862, and was subsequently sent back to Tennessee to serve as an army recruiter. By all accounts, Sarah and Sylvanius's marriage was happy, and the two spent as much time together as possible. After Sylvanius joined the military, whenever she could, Thompson assisted him in his recruitment efforts. Together they enlisted about 500 men.

The number may not seem so large until one considers that the Thompsons were recruiting members for the Union army in a state that had

This print, created between 1862 and 1865, is entitled *Entertaining Federal Soldiers.* Women served beverages to newly recruited Union soldiers in Baltimore, Maryland, during the Civil War. Some of the first bloodshed of the conflict occurred in Baltimore on April 19, 1861, when Union soldiers arrived at a train station and were attacked by Southern sympathizers. Twelve civilians and four soldiers were killed.

declared its loyalties to the Confederacy. They had to recruit in secret through a network of trust-worthy friends and acquaintances. When a sufficient number of men had signed up to serve, Sylvanius would provide them with a confidential meeting place and time. They would then travel in secret across the state line to Kentucky, where the men were sworn in to the Union army.

Thompson assisted Sylvanius on other assignments too, and she later wrote about the bond of trust that existed between them:

> [Sylvanius] came to help the union men escape from the wrath of the enemy and he had to stay in a secret place and keep himself hid. As a matter of course, someone had to help him and as he had more confidence in me than anyone else, he asked me to aid him.[1]

While on a dispatch to deliver a message to General Ambrose Burnside, who was stationed at the time in Knoxville, Tennessee, Sylvanius was captured. He was transported to Belle Island Prison in Richmond, Virginia, where he managed to escape after a few months. He soon returned to Tennessee, where he rejoined his regiment.

In January 1864, while on another delivery mission for the general, Sylvanius was captured again, this time by Confederate soldiers under General John Hunt Morgan. But Sylvanius would not be sent back to prison for a second offense; he was executed instead.

Though Thompson was immediately heartbroken by the news of her husband's death, his passing later inspired her. In a letter she wrote long after the end of the war, she recalled Sylvanius's

This image depicts Confederate soldiers guarding Union prisoners of war at a camp on Belle Island. Belle Island was located in the James River near Richmond, Virginia. No barracks were ever built for the prisoners. There were tents to sleep in, but not nearly enough for all of the prisoners. Body lice was rampant, and many men died from exposure or disease.

death: "While returning from a mission, he was captured by Morgan's guerrillas and shot. Having thus been widowed, I devoted all my strength and energy to aid the cause."[2] Thompson continued working for the Union, recruiting soldiers and delivering dispatches, but when she found out that her husband had died, she swore she would make the Confederacy pay for his death.

She didn't have to wait long. Less than a year after her husband was shot, Thompson heard through the grapevine that General Morgan had recently arrived in Greenville. Morgan was well known for his use of guerrilla tactics to make daring raids on Union-held cities in both the North and South, and he had a bad reputation with many Union loyalists. Thompson wasn't the only one who wanted him dead.

Wherever General Morgan went, he wreaked havoc, and the Union could not have been more delighted when he was captured during the summer of 1863. According to David Ray Skinner, "After several months of prison life, he and several other officers devised a plan to tunnel out of the prison. The plan succeeded and in November 1863, Morgan and six of his men escaped."[3] Explanations differ as to

This is a souvenir engraving of Confederate army general John Hunt Morgan (1825–1864). It is very similar to a portrait published in *Harper's Weekly* shortly before Morgan's execution. Both during and after the war, images of famous generals, battles, and war heroes were sold as mementos to the general public.

why Morgan showed up in Greenville a year after his escape. Some accounts say that he was there with 1,600 of his men, preparing for another raid. Others point out that he was there "to clear his name from accusations that he had been involved in the robbery of a civilian bank in Mt. Sterling, Kentucky."[4] Whatever Morgan's reasons were, while he was in Greenville, he stayed with the Williamses, family friends who lived in a large mansion near the center of town. His arrival in Greenville was newsworthy, and it wasn't long before Thompson knew exactly where he was staying.

Not knowing how long Morgan would remain in Greenville, Thompson immediately began working on a plan to reveal his whereabouts to a large force of federal cavalry stationed just outside of town. However, she would first have to figure out a way to get past the Confederate soldiers guarding all roads out of town.

Luckily, Thompson was acquainted with a Confederate captain whose family lived in Greenville. Thompson asked him if he could obtain permission from one of the sentries to let her pass so she could milk one of the cows grazing nearby. Recalling the event in a diary, Thompson wrote, "I promised I would give him some milk when I returned and he told the guard to pass me out and pass me in."[5]

Office of the Commissioner of Claims.
Washington D.C. April 13th 1876.
        No. 22,258.
Sarah E. Thompson. Tenn.
Late Lieut. 10th Michigan 13th Cav all at Washington. Edward J Brooks, says" I know that she was the person who conveyed the information to us of the presence of Gen! Morgan in Greenville, the information resulting in the move upon Greenville and the death of Morgan, and the defeat of his Command. She was very often engaged as a Spy, she had been a short time before the death of Morgan, up as far as Wytheville, Va, on a spying expedition for us and brought her information to us at Strawberry Plains, and returned to Greenville, having been very seriously injured by the fall of her horse when rebels were in pursuit of her, as so reported to us,"

This April 13, 1876, letter from Union lieutenant E. J. Brooks to the Office of the Commissioner of Claims confirms the death of General Morgan and discusses Thompson's activities as a spy. The letter is from the Special Collections Library at Duke University in North Carolina.

Once she passed the guard, Thompson raced to a friend's house where she was able to borrow a horse. It was near midnight when she finally reached the camp. Awoken from sleep, Major General Alvan Gillem, the commander in charge, did not at first believe her report on Morgan's whereabouts. However, two officers on his staff confirmed that Thompson had been a reliable source of information in the past.

One hundred Union cavalrymen were immediately selected to ride into Greenville and recapture Morgan. Although Thompson must have been exhausted from the long and dangerous trip, she did not want to leave anything to chance by staying behind. Concerned that Morgan might leave the mansion before they returned, Thompson had made arrangements so that he could not escape undetected. Besides, Thompson was not about to miss witnessing the demise of the man who was at least partially responsible for her husband's death.

Larry G. Eggleston writes: "General Morgan was still asleep when the Union troops swept in to Greenville just prior to dawn. When the alarm was sounded by one of the sentries, Morgan was shaken awake by his guards. Quickly donning a pair of pants over his nightclothes, he hurried downstairs and asked Mrs. Williams where the Yankees were. 'Everywhere,' she replied."[6]

As Thompson suspected, Morgan was tipped off that the cavalry was coming and escaped before their arrival. As she recorded in her diary, Thompson was well prepared for the event. She recalled, "I paid a colored woman 25 [cents] to watch him and when I got back and found he had gone, I went back and asked her where he was."[7]

Indeed, the woman had done just as Thompson had asked and informed her that Morgan was hidden in a nearby vineyard. Thompson told the nearest Union soldier she could find, and within minutes Morgan was discovered. He refused to surrender and was shot and killed on the spot.

In the days following Morgan's death, chaos ensued, and Thompson was captured and held prisoner in her own home. Her captors threatened to hang her. They told her that her hanged body would be displayed for at least three days. But Thompson was rescued by members of the Union army, and because there was a reward for her capture, she left Greenville. First, she relocated to Knoxville, Tennessee, then to Cleveland, Ohio, where she served as a nurse until the war ended.

In a letter she wrote to U.S. secretary of the treasury John Sherman in 1879, Thompson summarized her wartime accomplishments.

> I obtained [information] concerning the actual and intended movements, strength and disposition of the rebel forces. [I] led union men desiring to enlist into the federal lines. [I] was the frequent bearer of secret dispatches between commanding officers. [I] gave Federal officers the information of Morgan's presence in Greenville, which lead to his defeat and death. [I] was given three hours notice to abandon my home and proclaimed a Union spy by [Confederate president] Jefferson Davis, who authorized a reward for my arrest. After which, I served as a nurse in Knoxville and Cleveland, where I remained as a nurse until the close of the war.[8]

Judging from her letter to the Honorable John Sherman, Thompson wrote asking for financial assistance, but none was made available to her at that time. After the war, she supported herself by giving lectures in Northern cities about her wartime activities, but there was little money to be made speaking about such accomplishments.

Perhaps in an effort to make the lives of her children more secure, Thompson married Orville

★ARMY NURSE'S PENSION★ Special Act.
ACT AUG. 5, 1892.

CERTIFICATE DIVISION.   3—165 b.   NOTICE OF ISSUE AND FEES.

Department of the Interior,
BUREAU OF PENSIONS,

Washington, D. C., May 7, 1898.

Madam:

Herewith is transmitted a certificate No. 964170 for Orig. pension, issued this day in your favor, accompanied by a voucher for the amount now due and payable thereon.

You should execute the voucher in accordance with the printed instructions, and return it to the pension agent at Washington who will then send directly to your address, a check for the pension due.

Your recognized attorney is No Atty

of _____ whose fee

is _____ dollars, which is payable by the pension agent.

Very respectfully,

H. Clay Evans
Commissioner.

Sarah E. Cotton
Wash.
D. C.

This pension certificate was awarded to Sarah E. Thompson on May 7, 1898. "Army Nurse's Pension" is stamped at the top, and the certificate is from the Department of the Interior. The notice is signed by Sarah E. Cotton, the commissioner of the Bureau of Pensions.

J. Bacon a year after the war ended. They had two children, but the marriage was short and ended with Orville's early death from an illness.

On her own once again and now with four children to support, Thompson struggled to make ends meet. In an effort to receive compensation for her services during the war, Thompson repeatedly wrote letters to influential members of the government and the military pleading her case. Her efforts paid off in the form of a clerical job with the Treasury Department, for which she was paid $600 per year.

In the 1880s, Thompson married James Cotton, who, like her previous two husbands, died soon after they were wed. Her efforts to receive compensation for her service during the war finally paid off in 1899, when, by special action of the fifty-fifth Congress, Thompson was granted a pension of $12 per month.

When she turned sixty-five, she retired from her government position. She was living with her son Orville Bacon Jr. at the time and was going to visit him at his job one afternoon when she was hit by a trolley. Thompson died from her injuries on April 21, 1909, and was buried in the Washington, D.C., Arlington National Cemetery with full military honors.

ELIZABETH VAN LEW

As a Union spy, Elizabeth Van Lew was unique. She was different from her contemporaries because of her upper-class Southern upbringing, which was advantageous in carrying out her covert operations.

Van Lew was born on October 12, 1818, in Richmond, Virginia, to an affluent, slave-owning family. From a young age, however, she was outspoken in her distaste of slavery. When her father died, she released the family's slaves from bondage. During the Civil War, she created a wide and complex

This is a *carte de visite* of Elizabeth Van Lew by photographer A. J. De Morat. Cartes de visite were small prints mounted on cards that allowed relatives and friends to exchange portraits. Unlike earlier photographs, they could easily be sent through the mail. Their small size also made them relatively inexpensive.

spy ring that provided a wealth of information for the Union army.

Despite her sympathy with the Union's cause, Van Lew never strayed from viewing herself as a Southern woman at heart. Her bipartisan outlook won her few friends. After the war, she was largely shunned by the people of Richmond.

Van Lew was the eldest child of John and Elizabeth Van Lew. She was one of the three children fathered by John, a native of Long Island, New York. John Van Lew left Long Island after his business failed and moved south to Richmond, Virginia, where he and a partner began a hardware business. Because the store was unique to the South, it was very successful.

Soon the Van Lews became wealthy and were well regarded in Richmond society.

Van Lew's mother, the former Elizabeth Louis Baker, was born in Philadelphia, where Van Lew was sent for her formal education. It is possible that there Van Lew first formed her opinions about slavery, to which she was opposed from an early age. "Slave power degrades labor," she wrote in

This is the Elizabeth Van Lew mansion in Richmond, Virginia. The mansion served as a meeting place for other Richmond Unionists. The home was demolished in 1911; an elementary school currently occupies the spot.

her journal, "Slave power is arrogant, is jealous and intrusive, is cruel, is despotic, not only over the slave, but over the community, the state."[1]

However, the beginnings of her heartfelt views were probably in place long before she entered any classroom. In her journal, Van Lew describes herself as "tolerant and uncompromising, but liberal, quick in feeling, and ready to resent what seemed to me wrong—quick and passionate but not bad tempered or vicious. This has made my life sad and earnest."[2] As such, Van Lew was never shy about informing those who knew her about her opinions. She frequently argued about the topic with her father, insisting that he free the nine slaves owned by the family.

Van Lew's pleas were ignored, but youth was on her side. When Van Lew's father died when she was in her mid-twenties, she promptly liberated the family's slaves. Some of them left, while others stayed on as paid workers. Using her inheritance money, she also set about freeing the relatives of those who were now employed by her.

Though a proud Virginian, Van Lew was dismayed when talk of secession rumbled through Richmond. It was around this same time that Van Lew began her pro-North activities by corresponding with federal officials and letting them know about happenings in Richmond.

When Virginia seceded in the spring of 1861, Van Lew and her mother were called upon to aid the Confederate cause. They flatly refused but were eventually forced to comply under the duress of personal threats. The henchmen who pushed her into service would have done better to ban Van Lew forever from partaking in any wartime activities instead of inserting her in the middle of them. Rather than sitting quietly at home, Van Lew now had a direct line on confidential information about the Confederacy's war plans, which she promptly turned over to the federal government.

Before the start of the war, Van Lew and her mother fulfilled their obligations by bringing religious books to the camps. After the first land battle of the war, the Battle of Big Bethel, on June 10, 1861, federal prisoners began to arrive in Richmond. Van Lew was struck by the poor treatment they were receiving and volunteered to supply them with food, clothing, and medicine. While bringing in supplies, she also managed to gather intelligence from the prison guards as well as the prisoners, who had been brought through Confederate lines on the way to Richmond.

This photo depicts an 1864 Civil War camp at Brandy Station, Virginia. Union soldiers stand in front of the company kitchen. Union soldiers were entitled to receive rations of 12 ounces (340 grams) of pork or bacon or 20 oz. (567 g) of fresh or salt beef; 22 ounces (624 g) of soft bread or flour; and 16 ounces (454 g) of hard bread or 20 ounces (567 g) of cornmeal.

The people of Richmond grew increasingly angry with her visits to enemy prison camps, but Van Lew was undeterred. The act of freeing the family's slaves along with her sympathy for the Union military earned her the nickname of Crazy Bet among the townspeople. Van Lew viewed the moniker as an advantage and played up the role of the "crazy" old lady whenever she was in public. While the residents of Richmond may have disliked her activities, a disheveled woman who mumbled loudly while going about her errands was less likely of being suspected of committing espionage.

While the city's residents entertained themselves by gossiping about Crazy Bet, she kept herself busy by widening the reach of her covert operations and reporting to her Union contacts under the code name Babcock. In addition to the work she carried out with her mother at the prisons, Van Lew also gathered information through a wide network of her own employees and slaves who were still in bondage. Van Lew wrote of these slave activities: "Information was delivered by servants carrying baskets of eggs. One egg in each basket was hollow and contained her notes, which she had torn into small pieces. In addition, notes were carried in the soles of the servants' shoes."[3]

Mary Elizabeth Bowser was one of the Van Lews' servants. Elizabeth had sent her to Philadelphia to the Quaker School for Negroes. Since Van Lew now needed Bowser to help her in her spying activities, she convinced a friend to allow Bowser to work Confederate functions at President Jefferson Davis's mansion. After a few of these events at the mansion, Jefferson's wife thought that Bowser would be excellent as a staff servant. Bowser worked for the Davis family from 1863 until the end of the Civil War. According to several accounts, she had a photographic memory and, while there, put it to good use reporting on the president's activities.

Van Lew also used her society connections to gather information on the Confederates. As a member of Richmond's upper class, she often hosted parties in her own home for Richmond's high-ranking Confederate officials and other elite families. The commander of a Richmond prison, Lieutenant David H. Todd, whose half sister was the wife of Abraham Lincoln, was one of Van Lew's closest friends. After Lieutenant Todd was reassigned, she befriended his replacement commander, who, along with his family, became boarders living in the Van Lew mansion.

Though those who acted covertly often had a reputation for reporting information that was exaggerated, Van Lew was known for the accuracy of the information she gathered. Her solid reputation meant that she communicated with "some of the Federal government's highest-ranking officers, including George H. Sharp, chief of the U.S. Bureau of Military Information, Benjamin Butler, commander of the Army of the James, George G. Mead, commander of the Army of the Potomac, and Ulysses S. Grant, commander of the Union forces."[4]

Despite Van Lew's awareness that she was being watched closely by operatives for the Confederates, she remained fearless, carrying on a number of risky operations, including a spy ring, within the confines of her home. The mansion was a well-known safe house in which Van Lew frequently hid runaway slaves and prisoners en route to the North. Among the many sections of her house was a large secret room that once hid more than 100 men.

In April 1865, after repeated attempts, the federal army overtook Richmond. In an act that could be considered either extremely brave or extremely foolish, Van Lew had an American flag smuggled through the lines, and when Richmond surrendered, she and her servants climbed up to the roof of the house and raised it. It was the first flag to be displayed in Richmond since the start of the war.

The sight of the flag enraged Van Lew's neighbors, and many of them gathered on her lawn and shouted threats at her. She defiantly opened her door and yelled, "General Grant will be here in one hour. I know all of you, and if you harm me or my property your homes will be burned to the ground by noon."[5]

On April 3, 1865, the Union army arrived in Richmond. Not forgetting all her vital contributions, General Grant offered his thanks during a

This image from *Harper's History of the War* is entitled *Marching on Richmond*. A popular Union song of the time was called "Marching onto Richmond," and the chorus is "Then tramp away/While the bugles play/We're marching onto Richmond/Our flag shall gleam/In the morning beam/From many a spire in Richmond."

visit to her home, where he stationed several soldiers to guard her and the mansion.

Van Lew was ecstatic. In her journal she wrote, "What a moment! The chains, the shackles fell from thousands of captives. Civilization advanced a century. Justice, truth, humanity were vindicated. Labor was now without manacles, honored and respected. Oh, army of my country, how glorious was your welcome!"[6]

Following the conflict, General George H. Sharp proposed that Van Lew be appropriated $15,000 for her efforts during the war. In a letter, he wrote about Van Lew's "system of correspondence in cipher by which specific information asked for by General [Grant] was obtained."[7]

The Van Lew family received less compensation for their efforts. In 1869, fifteen days after Grant was inaugurated as president, he appointed Van Lew postmaster of Richmond. She received an annual salary of $1,200, which she sorely needed as she often used her own funds to finance her spying activities. As a result, she had been nearly penniless by the end of the war.

The citizens of Richmond resented Van Lew's appointment, and as more information on her wartime activities surfaced, her unpopularity increased. She spent the final years of her life ostracized by those around her. In a letter to John H. Forbes, a former Union solder who helped her financially in her later years, she wrote, "I live here in the most perfect isolation with my niece. We have no friendly visits, except that once or twice a year two families call. You know the women have never forgiven me."[8] When her mother died in 1875, she wrote another acquaintance that she did not have enough friends to serve as pallbearers.

Van Lew died on September 25, 1900, at the age of eighty-two. At the time she was destitute. Her funeral was attended by a handful of family members, servants, and relatives of the Union soldiers she had helped during the war. She was buried in Shockoe Hill Cemetery in Richmond. Years later, relatives of Colonel Paul Revere (Paul Revere's grandson, whom she had helped escape from prison) purchased a headstone, which reads, "She risked everything that is dear to man—friends, fortune, comfort, health and life itself. All for one absorbing desire of her heart—that slavery might be abolished and the Union preserved."[9]

It is likely that she would appreciate the kind words that grace her headstone. The journal entries Van Lew wrote following the war indicate that she felt her wartime efforts were not appreciated. One of her final journal entries reflects these mixed feelings.

> If I am entitled to the name of "Spy" because I was in the secret service, I accept it willingly; but it will hereafter have to my mind a high and honorable signification.

For my loyalty to my country I have two beautiful names—here I am called, "Traitor," farther North a "spy"—instead of the honored name of "Faithful."[10]

MARY ELIZABETH BOWSER

Throughout the Civil War, slaves and freed slaves were an invaluable source of information about Confederate wartime activities. As house servants and even as field workers, they often had an inside view on the lives of some of the South's most prominent military and government leaders. However, for a variety of reasons, there is scant information on the lives of these slaves, much less the covert acts they committed in the name of winning the freedom of their people.

Mary Elizabeth Bowser, a freed slave, is one of the few whose activities have been recorded. The fact that Bowser has gained a small amount of fame for her missions is not surprising. After all, Bowser achieved the ultimate coup—during the Civil War, she acted as a spy within the home of none other than Jefferson Davis, the president of the Confederacy!

Bowser, whose surname was Van Lew before she married, was born sometime around 1839 to parents who were slaves on a plantation owned by John Van Lew, father of Elizabeth Van Lew. (One account reports, "Bowser was purchased by the Van Lew family to be a playmate for Van Lew's oldest daughter, Elizabeth."[1]) The exact date of her birth is not known. Lacking the rights of citizens, slaves were viewed as less important

This is a portrait of Major General Jefferson Davis, who became president of the Confederacy. After the war, Davis settled on the Mississippi Gulf Coast and wrote an autobiography, *The Rise and Fall of the Confederacy.* He died on December 6, 1889, in New Orleans.

than whites, and their slave masters saw little reason to record the official details of their lives.

When Van Lew died in 1843, his oldest daughter, Elizabeth, who was outspoken in her distaste of the institution of slavery, freed all nine of the family's slaves. Most left the Van Lew plantation, though some, including Mary Elizabeth Bowser's parents, chose to remain as hired farmhands and house servants. Mary Elizabeth, who was a young girl at the time, stayed with her parents. When she turned ten, Van Lew sent her to be educated at the Quaker School for Negroes in Philadelphia.

Not long after she finished her schooling, she married Wilson Bowser, a free black man. The wedding ceremony took place on April 16, 1861, at St. John's Church in Richmond, in front of an audience of white parishioners. This arranged union of two blacks in front of a white audience was very unusual in the South.

At the time of Bowser's marriage, though the Civil War had just begun, Elizabeth Van Lew had already been providing the federal government with a steady stream of information about the Confederacy's military plans and actions near Richmond, as was explained in the previous chapter. When the war began, Van Lew simply

SLAVE MARRIAGES.

Passed Upon by the District of Columbia Circuit Court.

WASHINGTON, D. C.—In the District of Columbia circuit court to-day Judge Bradley decided, in a case involving property willed by free Afro-American parents, formerly slaves, to their children, that where there was no proof of actual marriage between the slave parents within the limits of time allowed by an act of congress of 1879 and various acts of state legislatures legitimizing children born of slaves such children were not entitled to inherit as legitimate issue. The case, besides being of general interest, is of importance to many property holders in the District of Columbia. Valuable property in this city is involved through its former ownership by colored men, as to whose legal marriage and the rights of dowry of their wives no satisfactory evidence could be obtained. Much of this property has been transferred in recent years, and to minimize the chances of litigation through clouded titles arising from its former ownership by children of slaves, or freed men, careful speculators have taken the precaution to have it pass by technical purchase through the hands of numerous wealthy citizens before deeding it to the actual purchaser. By this means a bulwark of responsibility is imposed by between any embarrassing and expensive litigation.

Housed in the Ohio Historical Center Archives, this clipping from the *Cleveland Gazette* reports a ruling made in the District of Columbia Circuit Court by Judge Bradley, who ruled that because there was no legal proof of slave marriages, free African Americans could not pass on their property to their children. The institution of slavery created many such injustices for African Americans.

expanded what was already a large network of spies and operatives.

Details about how Bowser became a spy for Van Lew are sketchy. The two remained close after Bowser completed her education, though it is not clear where Bowser was living or working when Van Lew called on her to become a part of her spy network. In any case, given that Bowser was a free woman married to a free man, it is a testament to her commitment to end slavery as well as her trust in Van Lew that she would agree to take on such a dangerous role.

It is not clear who came up with the idea to plant Bowser as a servant spy in the Richmond home of Confederacy president Jefferson Davis. It is known, however, that in 1862 Bowser and Van Lew put the plan into action. Though Van Lew herself wasn't friendly with the Davises, she was well acquainted with several people who were frequent guests at their home. Van Lew knew of one such visitor who was a Union sympathizer, and she managed to persuade her to take Bowser to assist at functions at the Davis mansion. Though Bowser was intelligent and well educated, all agreed that she would arouse less suspicion if she took on the role of a slow-witted and obedient servant.

After a few events at the mansion, the friend encouraged Davis's wife, Varina Davis, to hire Bowser as a servant. Varina Davis agreed, and Bowser assisted the Davis family from 1863 until just before the end of the war.

While Bowser cleaned and cooked, she also waited on Jefferson Davis and his military leaders. In doing so she was able to read war dispatches and overhear conversations about the movements and strategies of Confederate troops. She memorized this information and told it to other spies who coded it and sent it to General Ulysses S. Grant and General Benjamin Butler, "'greatly enhancing the Union's conduct of the war,' according to the

This is a portrait of Varina Jefferson Davis, wife of Jefferson Davis. Varina was only seventeen when she met the thirty-six-year-old Jefferson. She wrote to her mother about him, "He impresses me as a remarkable kind of man, but of uncertain temper, and has a way of taking for granted that everybody agrees with him . . . yet he is most agreeable and has a peculiarly sweet voice . . ."

account assembled by the U.S. Army Military
Intelligence Corps Hall of Fame."[2]

Very little is known about where Bowser went
or what she did after the war. The date and place
of her death are unknown, which reflects both her
status as a black woman and her work as an
undercover agent.

In an effort to protect those who were part of
her espionage network, Van Lew recorded neither
the activities nor the names of her operatives in the
journal she kept during the war. Further confound-
ing efforts to find written proof of her activities,
Van Lew asked that the War Department destroy
all of the messages she had sent during the war.
While Van Lew's decision to keep Bowser's actions
secret was no doubt a wise one, the lack of written
proof led to some controversy as to whether
Bowser had actually acted as a spy within the
Davis household.

When her former Richmond home was opened
as the Confederate Museum in 1896, Varina Davis
spoke fondly of her faithful slaves, but said nothing
about the issue of treachery and spies. However,
after Van Lew's death in 1900, stories regarding
Bowser's activities in the Davis house resurfaced,
and perhaps hoping to put them to rest for good,

Varina Davis wrote to museum head Isabel Maury and denied the rumor of successful espionage. In a note dated April 17, 1905, written from her New York hotel, Davis discussed the subject.

> My daughter has sent me your letter of inquiry to know if I had in my employ an educated negro woman whose services were "given or hired by Miss Van Lew" as

This is a photograph of the Jefferson Davis estate taken in 1905. In the 1890s, the house was saved from demolition by a group of Richmond women, who formed the Confederate Memorial Literary Society. The building was reopened as the Confederate Museum on February 22, 1896. Today it is a national historic landmark.

a spy in our house during the war. We never had any such person about us. I had no "educated negro" in my household. My maid was an ignorant girl born and brought up on our plantation who if she is living now, I am sure cannot read, and who would not have done anything to injure her master or me if even she had been educated. That Miss Van Lew may have been imposed upon by some educated negro woman's tales I am quite prepared to believe.

Very truly yours,
Varina Jefferson Davis[3]

When faced with the possibility that she was responsible for such a colossal blunder, it comes as no surprise that Davis hotly denied the stories. What she perhaps knowingly failed to address in her letter is the likelihood that her maid was none other than Bowser putting on a fine performance as "an ignorant girl,"[4] all the while gathering critical information on Confederate operations.

Despite Davis's denials, some of Bowser's activities were confirmed by Thomas McNiven, who owned a bakery in Richmond and, sometimes in cooperation with Van Lew, operated an espionage network. Though McNiven kept a journal, after his death it was destroyed by the executor of his will in the early 1900s. However, in 1952, his grandson Robert Waitt had the wisdom to record the memories of McNiven's wartime activities as told to him by McNiven's oldest daughter.

Regarding McNiven's network of operatives, his daughter recalled her father's description of Bowser: "Van Lew's colored girl, Mary, was the best as she was working right in Jefferson Davis's home and [she] had a photographic mind. Everything she saw on the Rebel president's desk she could repeat word for word. She made a point of always coming out to my wagon when I made deliveries at the Davis' home to drop information."[5]

Within Bowser's own family, little mention was made of her wartime activities. The desire to protect her even after her death is illustrated in a comment made by McEva Bowser (the wife of Mary's grandnephew) when asked by a cousin in the 1960s if she had ever heard of Mary Bowser. She replied, "No, never heard of her. Well, they don't ever talk about her 'cause she was a spy."[6]

According to McEva Bowser, she came across what appeared to be Bowser's diary when her husband's mother died.

> I was cleaning her room and I ran across a diary, but I never had a diary and I didn't even realize what it was. And I did keep coming across [references to] Mr. Davis. And the only Davis I could think of was the contractor who had been doing some work at the house. And the first time I came across it, I threw it aside and said I would read it again. Then I started to talk to my husband about it but I felt it would depress him. So the next time I came across it I just pitched it in the trash can.[7]

In spite of the lack of printed material confirming Bowser's service as a spy, the U.S. Army concluded that there was sufficient evidence to induct her into the Military Intelligence Corps Hall of Fame on June 30, 1995, for her duties during the Civil War: "Ms. Bowser certainly succeeded in a highly dangerous mission to the great benefit of the Union effort. She was one of the highest-placed and most productive espionage agents of the Civil War."[8]

HARRIET TUBMAN

Harriet Tubman, who was born a slave, is best known for helping other slaves gain their freedom. During the Civil War, it is estimated that she led more than 300 slaves to freedom along the Underground Railroad, which was a secret network that helped fugitive slaves find sanctuary in either the free states or Canada. Tubman's work as spy during the war is less known, but is certainly significant.

In her later years, Tubman would come to be called

This is a photograph of abolitionist Harriet Tubman (1820–1913) taken in 1870. Tubman escaped slavery by marrying a freeman and then helped hundreds of other slaves find their way to freedom via a string of safe houses and routes known as the Underground Railroad.

"the Moses of her people," a description that becomes more significant when one considers Tubman's humble beginnings. She was born in 1820, the last of eleven children, on a plantation in Maryland. Both of her parents, Harriet Greene and Benjamin Ross, were slaves owned by Edward Brodas. Tubman was named Araminta Ross and nicknamed "Minty" as a child, though as a teen she would change her name to Harriet, after her mother.

Even as a youngster, Tubman was expected to take on chores around her family's home and on the plantation. For a young girl who knew of no other life, it was not a difficult existence, especially since her family surrounded her.

According to Ann Petry, the love and security that her family provided her ended one day when, "before she knew what was happening, she was seated in a wagon, beside a strange white woman who was now her mistress. She had been hired out by the master, Edward Brodas."[1] Not surprisingly, Tubman was unhappy there and did her best be as uncooperative as possible. Her plan worked, and before long she was sent back to live with her own family on the plantation.

However, it wasn't the last time that Tubman was hired out to neighbors, and on many occasions her unruly behavior led to beatings and other forms of abuse. When she was fifteen years of age, Tubman sustained a severe head injury when an overseer hit her with a heavy weight when she attempted to block him from pursuing a runaway slave.

The injury was so severe that those who witnessed it were sure Tubman would die. However, under her mother's care, she slowly recovered, though never completely. A deep scar remained on her forehead, and throughout her life she suffered from pain and other difficulties related to the injury.

Not long after Tubman was well enough to work again, Brodas, the master of the plantation, died. In his will, Brodas decreed that none of his slaves were to be sold outside of the state of Maryland. Tubman was rented out to John Stewart, a lumber merchant. The job suited her not only because she was outside, but also because Stewart allowed her to keep some of the money she made when she took on extra work.

In 1844 or 1845, Tubman married John Tubman, a free black man. His status as a freeman encouraged Tubman to hire a lawyer to look into her own legal history. The lawyer unearthed evidence that her mother had been free since the death of a former owner. The evidence proved that Tubman should not have been born a slave.

This information made Tubman resentful. She began to contemplate her freedom.

When the heir to the Brodas estate died, rumors began to fly that the new owner would disregard Brodas's decree. Certain that her sale was imminent, Tubman suggested to her husband that they plan an escape to the North. Not only was he against the idea, but he told her that he would tell her master as soon as he discovered that she had escaped.

Tubman felt badly betrayed, but her husband's threat did not change her mind, except that from then on she plotted her escape in secret. In her first attempt to flee, she brought her three brothers with her, but not long into their journey, they grew scared and forced Tubman to return to the plantation. She was furious but kept her anger at bay and continued to plot her escape.

When the chance arose, Tubman took flight on her own. She made her escape via the Underground Railroad and, after several days of travel, arrived in Philadelphia as a free woman.

But Tubman's status wouldn't last long. In an effort to appease Southern plantation owners who were angered by the number of escaped slaves, the government passed the Fugitive Slave Act,

Paul Conners took this photograph of the Bethel AME Church in Providence, Rhode Island, on August 29, 1998. The church is thought to have been a possible stop on the Underground Railroad. It was founded in 1795 by the African Freedman's Society, which was led by Harriet Tubman.

which declared that by law escaped slaves were still considered to be slaves and could be captured and returned to their owners.

The new law did not frighten Tubman, much less cause her to emigrate to Canada, where escaped slaves could still live freely. Instead, she was inspired to return to Maryland to help guide other slaves to freedom. As the Civil War drew closer, despite the price on her head, she worked as a public speaker at abolitionist and women's' rights meetings.

In November 1860, shortly after Abraham Lincoln was elected president, South Carolina seceded from the Union. Knowing that war was imminent, Tubman, who was living in Boston at the time, let it be known that she was very much interested in helping the Union's cause.

In 1862, Governor Andrew of Massachusetts requested that Tubman act as a nurse and teacher to a large group of slaves in Beaufort, South Carolina, who had been left behind when their owners fled the advance of Union troops. This appointment marked Tubman's first official act in her career as a Union nurse, spy, and scout.

The following year, she was able to make use of her skills navigating unknown territories, both acting as a scout as well as organizing a group of black scouts and spies. Lead by Colonel James Montgomery, Tubman's first mission was as a scout on the Combahee River expedition. Their mission was to destroy the Confederate army's bridges and railroads with the goal of slowing down the enemy's ability to receive supplies.

Upon seeing the Union's boats advancing down the river, slaves who were working nearby rushed down to the riverside. About 800 slaves crowded the banks with their hands raised. They were all taken aboard boats and transported south to Beaufort.

Subsequently, Tubman was often sent into the rebel lines as a spy. Author Sarah Bradford interviewed Tubman at length for the book *Harriet Tubman: The Moses of Her People.* Bradford wrote: "[Tubman] has been in battle when the shot was falling like hail, and the bodies of dead and wounded men were dropping around her like leaves in autumn; but the thought of fear never seems to have had place for a moment in her mind. She had her duty to perform, and she expected to be taken care of till it was done."[2]

When the war ended, Tubman returned to Auburn, New York, where her parents lived in a home she had purchased for them not long after she had secured their freedom in 1857. She brought with her a bundle of letters and recommendations from officers for whom she had served. In one letter written by Colonel Montgomery, dated July, 6, 1863, he referred to her as "a most remarkable woman, and invaluable as a scout."[3]

In 1999, photographer Todd Dudek took this photograph of a roadside marker that notes Harriet Tubman's birthplace in Bucktown, Maryland. The sign was put up by the Maryland Civil War Centennial Commission and states that Tubman "served the Union Army as a nurse, scout, and spy."

Associated Press photographer Gail Oskin took this picture of the unveiling of the Harriet Tubman statue in the South End neighborhood of Boston, Massachusetts, on June 20, 1999. The statue is entitled *Step On Board*, and celebrates Tubman's courage as well as that of the slaves who were inspired to follow her and risk their own lives.

In 1869, Tubman married again. Her husband, Nelson Davis, was more than twenty years younger than she. He struggled with tuberculosis, which he contracted while serving in the Civil War. With her husband unable to work, Tubman repeatedly applied for a pension and back pay to reimburse her for those years she had served with the Union forces. In 1899, Tubman finally received a pension of $20 a month. Ironically, it was not for her services, but for being the widow of her second husband, who had died a decade before.

In the final years of her life, Tubman remained committed to the lives of people who struggled. In 1903, she turned her home over to a church in order for it to be used as a home for the poor and homeless. She lived there until she died at the age of ninety-two on March 10, 1913. Recognition of her service during the war came with her death, and she was given a military funeral with honors.

PAULINE CUSHMAN

5

Of all the women who had spied for the Civil War, Pauline Cushman was probably the most dramatic. Cushman was, in fact, an actress who launched her espionage career by offering a toast to Confederacy president Jefferson Davis just prior to a performance. It was just a ploy, and one that she used to ingratiate herself with Confederate sympathizers and, eventually, to pass through their lines unheeded in her quest for information.

Cushman was doubly effective as a Union spy

because she was born and spent much of her young life in the South. As a result Cushman was able to pass as a Southerner because of her accent and her understanding of Southern mannerisms.

The daughter of a Spanish tradesman, Cushman was born Harriet Wood on June 10, 1833, in New Orleans, where even as a child she had an

This sketch is titled *The Treasonable Toast at the Louisville Theatre*, and depicts Pauline Cushman (in men's attire) making her brilliantly deceptive toast to the Confederacy before a performance. A *New York Times* article later noted that "among the women of America who have made themselves famous since the opening of the rebellion, few have suffered more or rendered more service to the Federal cause than . . . Pauline Cushman, the female scout and spy."

adventurous spirit, preferring to play the rough-and-tumble games of boys. As a young girl, she had a reputation for being a skilled shooter and an expert horsewoman. When Cushman was in her teens, her family moved to Grand Rapids, Michigan.

Once there, she found that she had outgrown the activities that so entertained her as a young-ster. She grew restless and bored by Grand Rapids, then just a small frontier town located in a largely rural region. By the time Cushman was eighteen, she had had enough. She ran away to New York City to pursue a career in acting.

Soon after arriving in New York, she took on the stage name of Pauline Cushman and found a small degree of success as a stage actress. While in New York, she also fell in love with a musician and teacher named Charles Dickinson, who was also a member of the regimental band of the 41st Ohio Infantry.

The two married in 1853. Their wedding was held in a hotel in New Orleans, where they settled and had two children. When both of their children died in infancy, the couple moved to Cleveland, Ohio, where Dickinson enlisted as a soldier for the Union. Not nearly as durable as his wife, Dickinson was discharged because of illness

Famous Civil War photographer Mathew Brady took this photograph of Pauline Cushman in full military uniform around June 1864. The original negative is in the Meserve Collection of the Smithsonian Institution.

within months of enlisting. Within two years of the start of the war, Dickinson had died.

Without a husband or children, Cushman threw herself into her acting career and joined a touring theatrical company. While performing in Louisville, Kentucky, she was offered a challenge that she would use to catapult herself into the thick of the Civil War as a spy.

Charmed by her good looks and talent, several Confederates offered her $300 to toast Jefferson Davis and the Confederacy just before a performance one evening. It is not known whether her challengers knew of her sympathies with the Union and were perhaps testing her loyalty to the South (at the time, Louisville was occupied by the North, though most of its residents were Confederate sympathizers). Whatever their intentions, the quick-thinking Cushman saw an opportunity to take up the battle for the Union that her husband never lived.

Cushman immediately notified the local Union marshal with this news. Given her background, it was clear that she had the potential to do espionage work, but before she received the go-ahead, it was decided that she would have to take an oath of loyalty to the Union.

Cushman eagerly complied with the requirement, and the following night, she took the stage and proposed a toast to Jefferson Davis and the Confederacy. Fighting in the theater broke out following her announcement. Cushman was subsequently fired by the theater. She couldn't have been more delighted with this outcome and thus began her career as a Civil War spy.

Cushman's career in espionage was short, but productive. She informed on other spies and sympathizers, assisted army police, and reported useful information about troop movements, strategies, and supplies. As the number of missions Cushman completed grew, so did suspicion of her true intentions.

She was transferred to Nashville, Tennessee, where she worked for a general named William Rosencrans and spent several months with the Cumberland army. While General Rosencrans was preparing a campaign to drive Confederate general Braxton Briggs across the Tennessee River in 1863, Cushman was sent into Confederate lines to determine the whereabouts and abilities of the Tennessee army.

In 1865, the final year of the Civil War, time was running out for Cushman. Although she gathered important information for several weeks,

This wood engraving depicts the tents of Union general James H. Wilson's cavalry on a hill, 6 miles (9.7 km) from Nashville, Tennessee. It appeared in *Harper's Weekly* on December 31, 1864.

Confederate soldiers finally captured her. Using her skills as an actress, she feigned illness and, when the opportunity arose, managed to break away from her captors.

The escape was short-lived, and within days, the same soldiers captured her again. A search of Cushman's belongings revealed that she was in possession of drawings she had stolen from an army engineer. She was promptly arrested.

Weakened by fever, Cushman was too ill to attend her own trial. Her jailer kept her abreast of court proceedings. The court found her guilty and sentenced her to death by hanging with instructions that the sentence be carried out immediately.

Never one to give up easily, Cushman calmly plotted out her last deceit. In an odd show of sympathy, perhaps because she was a woman, the court granted Cushman a stay until she was fully recovered from her illness. Once again, falling back on her flair for the dramatic, Cushman was able to convince her captors that she was ill well after she was on the road to recovery.

Her ploy was starting to wear thin when the Union army invaded Cumberland, Tennessee, the city in which she was being held. General William Rosecrans's advance guard spared her life as the Confederates retreated. She was freed, and after her rescue, Secretary of War Edwin Stanton appointed her a major in the U.S. Army and President Lincoln referred to her as "the little major."[1] Cushman was soon appreciated throughout the North.

In the years following the war, her heroic efforts were described in several articles and books, including *The Life of Pauline Cushman*, written from

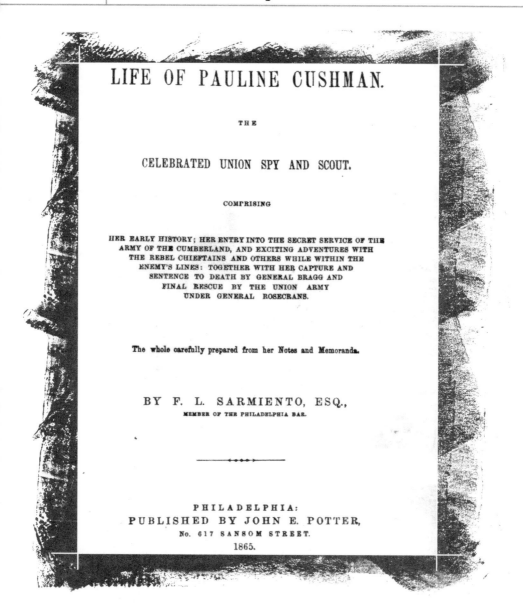

LIFE OF PAULINE CUSHMAN.

THE

CELEBRATED UNION SPY AND SCOUT.

COMPRISING

HER EARLY HISTORY; HER ENTRY INTO THE SECRET SERVICE OF THE
ARMY OF THE CUMBERLAND, AND EXCITING ADVENTURES WITH
THE REBEL CHIEFTAINS AND OTHERS WHILE WITHIN THE
ENEMY'S LINES: TOGETHER WITH HER CAPTURE AND
SENTENCE TO DEATH BY GENERAL BRAGG AND
FINAL RESCUE BY THE UNION ARMY
UNDER GENERAL ROSECRANS.

The whole carefully prepared from her Notes and Memorands.

BY F. L. SARMIENTO, ESQ.,
MEMBER OF THE PHILADELPHIA BAR.

PHILADELPHIA:
PUBLISHED BY JOHN E. POTTER,
No. 617 SANSOM STREET.
1865.

This is the title page of the book *Life of Pauline Cushman.*
It was published by John E. Potter in Philadelphia in 1865,
and Cushman's notes and "memorands" were compiled by
Ferdinand Sarmiento, a lawyer from Philadelphia. Today scholars
believe that some events described in the book are exaggerated.

Cushman's notes by Ferdinand Sarmiento in 1865. Many of the book's more colorful details have been discounted in recent years. For example, though the story of Cushman starting her career by offering an onstage toast may be a dramatic one, it is believed by some that she was "already a secret agent when she toasted Jefferson Davis and the Confederacy from a Louisville stage."[2]

After the war, Cushman returned to the stage with limited success. She also capitalized on her experience as a spy. Under the name of Spy of the Cumberland, she began lecturing. By 1872, her speaking engagements brought her to California. Cushman was well known for her fiery temper, which came to light when several California newspapers questioned her identity as a former spy. Upon learning of their doubts, she reportedly "threatened to horsewhip one of the paper's editors."[3]

Struggling financially, Cushman applied for a pension based on her service as a secret agent during the war. Despite being commissioned a major, she received only a monthly pension because of the time that her husband had served.

She married August Fitcher the same year she arrived in San Francisco. Her government pension ceased when she remarried, and within seven years her second husband died. Not long after his death, she took a third husband, though this union did not last either. After several unhappy years, she left him.

Cushman's affinity for an adventurous life eventually caught up with her. Eking out an existence as a maid, she became addicted to morphine. Several accounts describe her death on December 2, 1893, as caused by suicide, however, the local coroner ruled that the cause of death was "from morphine taken, not with suicidal intent, but to relieve pain."[4]

The Grand Army of the Republic gave Cushman a full military funeral, which was attended by more than 800 veterans. She was buried in a military cemetery with a headstone that read, "Pauline Cushman, Federal Spy and Scout of the Cumberland."[5]

SARAH EMMA EDMONDS

Not all Civil War spies were born in America. One of the war's most well-known spies, Sarah Emma Edmonds, was born in Canada. Her father, Isaac Edmonson, immigrated to New Brunswick from Scotland in the early 1800s and eventually married Elizabeth Leeper, who came to Canada via Ireland.

Elizabeth bore six children, five girls and one boy. Sarah, who would be known by her middle name, Emma, was born in December 1841 and was the youngest girl. She and her siblings attended

Emma Edmonds found great inspiration in the heroine of this book *Fanny Campbell: The Female Pirate Captain.* Women led restricted lives in the nineteenth century and were often pressured into arranged marriages and prevented from working outside the home. Stories like that of Campbell's inspired women who wished to break out of society's restrictive roles.

school at a one-room schoolhouse, and each Sunday the family attended an Anglican church.

Edmonds was a spirited little girl. In addition to the hard work she did helping her father run his farm, she enjoyed swimming, riding horses, and hunting. Though it was common for farm girls to partake in all of these activities, Edmonds was much more active and mischievous than her siblings, including her younger brother. Recalling her childhood in a diary, she wrote, "I heard my mother once tell a Scotch Presbyterian clergyman that she was afraid I would meet with some violent death, for I was always in some unheard of mischief."[1]

Edmonds's friendly demeanor would lead her to make influential relationships throughout her life, but it was a chance meeting with a peddler who visited their farm that would change her view on her own destiny. Charmed by Edmonds, who generously invited him to stay for dinner, the peddler returned her kindness with the gift of a book, *Fanny Campbell: The Female Pirate Captain*. Edmonds immediately became entranced by the book's brave and daring hero. Sylvia Dannet writes:

> At the point in the book where the heroine, Fanny Campbell, in a plot to save her imprisoned lover, cut off her auburn curls, put on her blue jacket and "stepped into the freedom and glorious independence of masculinity," Emma flung her straw hat into the air and shouted in excitement. "Someday I will follow Fanny Campbell's example!"[2]

When Edmonds turned fifteen, she found herself being pursued by an older farmer who lived nearby. Edmonds was appalled by his advances as well as her father's approval of his actions and insistence that preparations be made for the two to wed. Edmonds's mother, however, sided with her daughter and made plans for her to leave the farm with a trusted friend just one day before the wedding. When Edmonds left her family behind, she also left her past behind, including changing her name from Edmonson to Edmonds.

For several years she lived with her mother's friend Annie Moffitt in Salisbury, a lively town in Canada located near the U.S. border. She worked in Moffitt's millinery shop and quickly became a favorite among its visitors.

Several years after her arrival, Edmonds learned that her father knew of her whereabouts and was planning to come and bring her back to the family farm. Terrified that he might still insist upon the marriage from which she had fled, she began to plan an escape that would free her from his influence forever.

Following the lead of her favorite storybook heroine, Edmonds made her escape dressed as a man. She wasn't content, however, to use her disguise just to run away. She took Fanny's lead one step further by assuming the full identity of a man. Known as Frank Thompson to her new friends and acquaintances, she took on a job as a Bible salesman. Her new identity must have been a good one, for within the company her reputation was only that of an excellent employee.

Maintaining her identity as a man, Edmonds eventually traveled to the United States, where she felt the opportunities to make money as a salesman were much better than in Canada. She ended up in Michigan, where she continued to sell Bibles.

When the Civil War began, Edmonds could have returned to Canada but instead chose to enlist in the army. Since she was vehemently opposed to slavery, there was never any question that she would enlist with the Union army.

When President Abraham Lincoln put out a call for volunteers, "Frank" went to the recruitment center in Flint, Michigan. While no one doubted that she was a man, she

This is a portrait of Emma Edmonds dressed as a man. Her fellow soldier Jerome Robbins saw through Edmonds's disguise but befriended her instead of exposing her identity. Robbins respected her fortitude and her ability to fight. He wrote in his journal, "Though never frankly asserted by her, it will be understood that my friend Frank is a female . . ." Robbins's tolerance was unusual for his time.

This is a photograph taken sometime between 1861 and 1865 of injured soldiers at the 1,000-bed Armory Square Hospital. One of the largest Civil War hospitals, it was located on the National Mall, where the National Air and Space Museum stands today.

was turned away because she did not meet the military's height requirement. She persisted and, several months after her first attempt, was drafted as a male nurse with the rank of private.

In July 1860, Edmonds received her first active duty assignment when her unit was called upon to fight in the First Battle of Bull Run. The outcome was a bloody one with many soldiers injured and killed. In the days to follow, Edmonds attended the wounded in a hospital located in the nation's capital.

When a soldier with whom she had become close was shot and killed, Edmonds was inspired to avenge his death by taking on a more active role in the military. When she heard that there was a vacancy for a spy in the Union's Secret Service division, she immediately applied for the position.

On her first mission, for which she was to enter into Confederate territory and gather information about the enemy's plans, she was not content to simply dress as a man. In an effort to arouse less suspicion, Edmond dyed her skin black with iodine, obtained a curly black wig, and transformed herself into a black man.

Later, Edmonds described her first day as a spy: "With a few hard crackers in my pocket and my revolver loaded and capped, I started on foot without even a blanket or anything which might create suspicion."[3] After a day of traveling south toward Richmond, Virginia, she encountered a half-dozen slaves who were responsible for bringing food and supplies to Confederate soldiers, also known as pickets, who were standing watch for advancing federal soldiers. When an officer approached her and

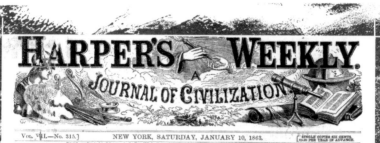

This wood engraving appeared in *Harper's Weekly* on January 10, 1863. It is entitled *Rebel Negro Pickets as Seen Through a Field Glass.* Many African Americans fought for the Confederacy, despite its promotion of slavery, out of loyalty to their home states or because they believed they and their families might be rewarded.

asked her to identify herself, she replied that she was a freeman on her way to Richmond in search of work.

Told by the officer that there were no free black men in Virginia, she was immediately put to work building a stone wall to protect Confederate soldiers from enemy fire. At night while everyone else slept, Edmonds took notes on the Confederate army's supplies and weapons.

After another day of hard work delivering water to soldiers, in the evening she was put to work carrying supplies to the pickets. In an effort to garner more information, Edmonds conversed for as long as possible with each soldier she visited. An officer noticed her dawdling and ordered her to take the post of a Confederate soldier who had recently been shot.

Edmonds took the post happily, knowing that it would provide the perfect opportunity to escape to the nearby federal camp. It was a cloudy, damp night. It began to rain, and the pickets on either side of her had taken shelter under trees. Noiselessly, grasping a Confederate rifle as a trophy, Edmonds walked through the woods toward the Union lines. She knew the federal pickets would fire on anybody moving toward them so she bedded down for the remainder of the night within hailing distance of the Union picket line.

Despite the danger, Edmonds's successfully completed mission only whetted her appetite to do more reconnaissance work. For her second assignment, she once again thought up an imaginative disguise. This time she dressed as an old Irish woman who made her living by traveling from city to city selling baked goods.

Not long after crossing into Confederate territory, she came upon an abandoned house in which she found a Confederate soldier on the verge of death. She comforted him as best she could in his final hours, and not long before he died, he requested that she deliver his watch and some papers to his commanding officer.

She set out for the deceased soldier's camp in the morning and soon saw a sentinel on the road ahead. Edmonds stopped to gather her thoughts, and while she rested she concluded that her story would be that much more believable if it appeared she had been grieving over the soldier's death. Ever the actress, she rubbed a pinch of pepper in her eyes, and within minutes, it appeared as though she had been crying for hours. In her diary she describes the event: "I took from my basket

Sarah Emma Edmonds stands proudly next to a horse in this engraving. When Edmonds was appointed as an aide to Colonel Orlando Poe, she also became the brigade's mail and dispatch carrier. Edmonds often put herself in danger and led her horse across swift running streams more than once to deliver the mail.

the black pepper and sprinkled a little of it on my pocket handkerchief, which I applied to my eyes."[4]

Her tears worked perfectly, and the soldier allowed her to pass without hesitation. In fact, so convinced was he of her sad tale that before she left he shared with her his unit's plans to fight off the enemy.

While waiting for the return of the dead soldier's commanding officer, she managed to gather more details on the Confederacy's plans. When the opportunity arose, she made her getaway laden with important information that would ultimately save the lives of many soldiers.

While in the military, Edmonds continued in her role as both spy and nurse as needed during battles. She also had a reputation for seeking out medical supplies and food for injured and under-fed troops.

When she wasn't needed as a nurse, she carried mail between camps. Near the start of the Second Battle of Bull Run, fought on August 29 and 30, 1862, her leg was badly injured when she was thrown from her horse while delivering the mail. Despite the fact that she could barely walk, she kept up her responsibilities as a mail carrier, only asking for assistance in mounting or dismounting her horse.

Whether Edmonds was cleverly disguised, as the list of her completed missions grew, it became increasingly likely that she would be recognized as a spy. Her last mission took place in Louisville, Kentucky. Though under Union command, the people who lived there supported the Confederacy, and Emma was sent there to dig up any information she could on counter-spy activity.

Not long after her arrival, she was hired as a clerk in a dry goods store, "where she proved to be such an efficient worker that her employer asked her if she would like to go out to the nearest Confederate camps and sell merchandise to the soldiers."[5] Her ability to ingratiate herself with strangers remained, and in no time she was able to uncover the names and whereabouts of three Confederate spies, two of whom were ultimately arrested.

In April 1863, Edmonds became severely ill. This time, she was unable to shake off her illness and carry on as she had done on so many past occasions. She requested a two-week leave, which was denied, leaving her with the sole option of

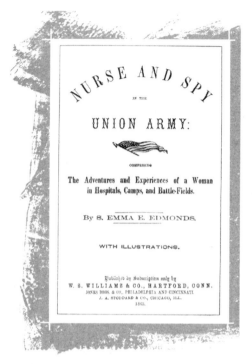

Edmonds's book, *Nurse and Spy in the Union Army: The Adventures and Experiences of a Woman in the Hospitals, Camps and Battlefields,* has sold more than 30,000 copies since its original publication. This is the title page of the 1865 edition.

convalescing in a hospital. Concerned that her true identity might be discovered, she made the decision to go AWOL and abandon her military career forever.

She wasn't quite ready to give up her disguise as Frank Thompson, though, and it was several more months before she would reclaim her female identity as Sarah Emma Edmonds. When she recovered her health and identity, she began work on a book that detailed her experiences during the war. Called *Nurse and Spy in the Union Army,* it was published in 1865 and became an immediate best-seller.

Shortly after her book was published, Edmonds met and married Linus Seely (which she later changed to Seelye), also a Canadian. She gave birth to three children and adopted two boys, though three of her children died young.

As the years passed by, she grew increasingly uncomfortable with the manner in which she had left behind her military career. Not only did she not receive any sort of wages or pension, Frank Thompson was still officially listed as a deserter. Twenty years after she left the army, Edmonds began a campaign to both receive any payment to which she was entitled as well as to have the status of deserter removed from "Frank's" records.

It took many years of hard work and persist-ence, but eventually Thompson was recognized for her service as a nurse in Company F, Second Regiment, Michigan Volunteer Infantry. "On April 2, 1889—seven years after she had first begun to seek government aid and the clearance of her name in the army records—[Thompson] was restored to honorable standings on the records of the War Department, granted an honorable dis-charge . . . back pay and bounty.'"[6]

Edmonds died at the age of fifty-seven due to complications from the illness that originally drove to her leave the military. Though she was first buried in La Porte, Texas, her remains were later moved to Washington Cemetery, a military burial place in Houston.

WOMEN OF CONVICTION

The women detailed in these chapters are just a handful of the many who served as Union spies, couriers, scouts, and informers during the Civil War. Unlike today, women during the Civil War were never officially hired by the military to carry out their acts of espionage, so there is little record of their service. The stories of the spies detailed in this book have survived because written records detailing their exploits were made either during the war or shortly thereafter.

This is a cabinet card portrait of Rebecca M. Wright that was created in Harrisburg, Pennsylvania, around 1889. The title of the print is "The loyal girl of Winchester, Miss Rebecca M. Wright, now Mrs. R. McP. Bonsal." Cabinet cards were similar to cartes de visite, but were larger. They were often tinted by hand.

There are other women, however, whose names are also worth mentioning. Generally, the details about their activities are scant, or they are known for committing a single act of bravery that in its own way helped to change the course of the war.

Prior to and during the war, Quakers were known for their opposition to slavery. Stops along the Underground Railroad were often homes and barns owned by Quakers. Once such Quaker was Rebecca Wright, a schoolteacher who lived in Winchester, Virginia. Writes Elaine Schneider: "One day after class, Rebecca opened her door to Thomas Laws, a black man posing as a peddler. Once within her home and away from prying eyes, the old man pulled a written message from his mouth. The paper read: 'Ms. Wright, I know that you are a loyal lady and still love the old flag. Can you inform me of the position of rebel troops and their probable intentions?' The note was signed by General Phillip Sheridan of the Union army."[1]

Until that time, Wright had not acted in any way as a spy or a scout, but she recalled overhearing a conversation between two Confederate soldiers while in town. She told the general what she knew, expecting that little would come of it. However, her scant information was the key to General Sheridan's decision to attack immediately, which enabled him to win the Third Battle of Winchester.

Anna Campbell, a Unionist who lived in northern Alabama "once rode seventy miles [113 km] in thirty-six hours to carry information to a Federal General."[2] Mary Pittman is one of only two known spies who began the war as a spy for the Confederacy and then switched allegiance.

Several women were arrested for spying, including Mary Walker, a medical doctor. According to Larry Eggleston, "At the age of twenty-nine, she applied for a commission with the U.S. army as a surgeon. At the time, there were few female doctors

A portrait of Dr. Mary Walker in a modified Union surgeon's uniform. Walker was the first woman to serve the U.S. Army as an Acting Assistant Surgeon. After the Civil War, Walker was recommended for the Medal of Honor by Generals William T. Sherman and George Thomas. She received the medal in 1866.

and her application was met with strong opposition and she was denied a commission."[3]

For the first two years, she volunteered as a nurse and was eventually appointed as a surgeon to the 52nd Ohio Volunteer Infantry Regiment. Accounts vary on whether Walker carried out spy missions. She made no mention of such activities in her own writing; however, as Elizabeth Leonard writes, "there is some evidence to suggest that Walker had been told by her superiors to use any access to the civilian community as a means of gaining whatever information she could about Confederate military maneuvers."[4]

Whatever may have been her intention, Leonard continues, "when she was traveling deep into enemy territory on April 10, 1864, Walker was stopped by a Confederate sentry and subsequently arrested."[5] Judging from the commentary on Walker following her arrest, the Confederates were far more put off by her status as surgeon and her masculine attire than by the possibility that she was a spy. In a letter detailing her capture, Captain B. J. Semmes wrote the following:

> We were all amused and disgusted too at the sight of a thing that nothing but the debased and depraved Yankee nation could produce—"a female doctor." She is fair, but not good looking and of course had tongue enough for a regiment of men. I was in hopes the General [Joseph E. Johnston] would have had her dressed in a homespun frock and bonnet and sent back to the Yankee lines, or put in a lunatic asylum.[6]

As there were no separate facilities for female prisoners, the Confederate military immediately attempted to arrange a prison exchange with the federal military. Her case languished, and Walker was held for four months before she was finally released.

Despite the many stories that have survived, much of the secret agent work that was carried out by women remained hidden. Women who acted as spies or scouts during the Civil War had little to gain by shedding light on their stories. As the biographies in this book demonstrate, even women whose service was recognized by military and political leaders struggled to receive any sort of compensation.

In addition, female spies who made their activities known were often judged as eccentric—if not freakish—for taking on work that was deemed inappropriate for women. And while the Union may have won the war, it did not win the hearts of most Confederates. As a result, it was downright dangerous for a Southerner who spied for the Union to reveal her activities after the war ended.

Certainly, many of the women involved in passing on information never viewed themselves as spies. They simply saw an opportunity to help the Union or Confederate cause. In the aftermath

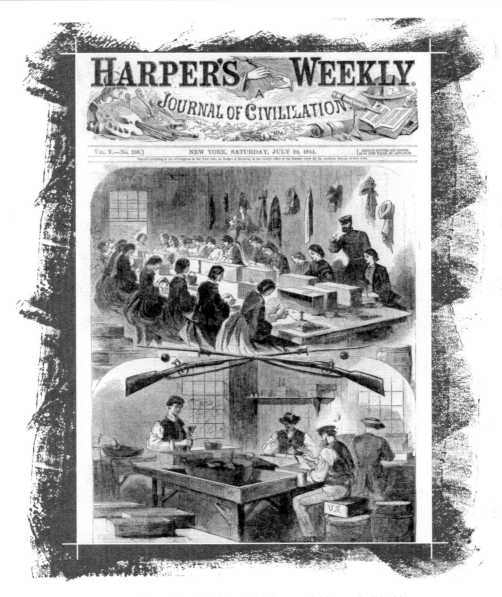

This image from the July 20, 1861, issue of *Harper's Weekly* shows male and female volunteers assembling ammunition at the United States arsenal in Watertown, Massachusetts.

of the war, those who were spies or operatives were not necessarily proud of their acts of deception, but rather viewed them as an unpleasant but necessary part of war. Indeed, in her later years, Emma Edmonds, one of the war's most accomplished spies, lamented her role as a spy and expressed a wish to edit her own diaries so that less emphasis could be placed on her undercover activities.

In looking at the many Civil War spy stories, it is difficult to categorize the women who chose to serve their country as secret agents. Their socioeconomic classes varied tremendously, ranging from slaves who owned nothing to women who were exceedingly wealthy. From a geographic perspective, Union spies claimed birthplaces that ranged from the Deep South to as far north as Canada. Many women who spied did so because they were opposed to slavery, though some simply believed in the preservation of the Union.

If nothing else, they were women of conviction. Like many women throughout history, they were not afraid to take a stand on issues in which they strongly believed. For all of them, there were great risks involved in their missions. Despite the substantial challenges and danger, these women were not cowed into submission and instead made the heroic choice not only to have an opinion but also to act on it.

TIMELINE

1777 – Vermont, still a colony, is the first government entity to abolish slavery.

March 1807 – Congress bans the importation of slaves into the country, effective on January 1, 1808.

1832 – Congress passes the Tariff Act of 1832, which reduces tariffs that favor the industrial economy of the North and damage the Southern agricultural economy. Still dissatisfied, several Southern states threaten to secede.

February 1850 – The Fugitive Slave Act is passed. It allows for the arrest or capture of fugitive slaves in all states, colonies, and territories.

1852 – Harriet Beecher Stowe publishes *Uncle Tom's Cabin* in response to the pro-slavery movement.

1857 – In the *Dred Scott* decision, the Supreme Court rules that blacks are not U.S. citizens, and thus slaveholders could travel openly with them to free states and territories without the fear of being sued.

1860 – Abraham Lincoln is elected the sixteenth president of the United States. In several states in the Deep South, his name is not included on the ballot. Shortly after his election, South Carolina secedes from the Union. Between 1860 and 1861, ten additional southern states secede and form the Confederacy.

February 1861 – Jefferson Davis is unanimously elected president of the Confederacy by state delegates.

April 1861	The Civil War begins when South Carolina's Fort Sumter is fired on by the Confederates.
June 1861	Tennessee, the final state to do so, secedes from the Union.
July 1861	Union forces under General McDowell are defeated at the First Battle of Bull Run.
November 1861	Lincoln appoints General George B. McClellan commander in chief of the Union armies.
June–July 1862	McClellan loses the Seven Days Battle east of Richmond.
July 1862	Lincoln promotes General Halleck to command all Union armies, demoting McClellan to command the Army of the Potomac.
September 1862	General McClellan wards off Confederate general Lee in the Battle of Antietam—the bloodiest day of fighting in American history.
January 1863	Lincoln formally signs the Emancipation Proclamation into law.
March 1864	Lincoln appoints General Grant commander of all U.S. armies.
November 1864	Lincoln is elected president for a second term.
January 1865	The House of Representatives passes the Thirteenth Amendment, which abolishes slavery.
April 1865	General Lee surrenders all Confederate forces under his command to General Grant at Appomattox Court House in Virginia.

Glossary

abolitionism A movement to abolish, or end, slavery. A person opposed to slavery was known as an abolitionist.

allegiance Devotion or loyalty to a person, group (such as a government), or cause.

bipartisan Of, consisting of, or supported by members of two political parties.

Civil War The conflict from 1861 to 1865 between the North (the Union) and the South (the Confederacy), which seceded from the Union. Also known as the War of the Rebellion and the War Between the States.

Confederacy The eleven Southern states that seceded from the United States in 1860 and 1861; also called the South. Members of the Confederacy were called Confederates.

demeanor A person's manner toward others.

demise The death of someone or something.

despot An autocratic or oppressive ruler; tyrant.

destitute Altogether lacking; without a means of financial support.

Emancipation Proclamation A declaration issued by President Abraham Lincoln that called for the end of slavery in the Confederate States. Issued on January 1, 1863, during the third year of the Civil War, it declared that "all persons held as slaves are and henceforward shall be free."

espionage The act of spying.

secede To withdraw from a group, such as a government.

sentry A guard, especially a soldier posted to prevent passage of unauthorized persons.

surname A person's last or family name as distinguished from a given name.

For More Information

The Civil War News
234 Monarch Hill Road
Tunbridge, VT 05077
(800) 777-1862
Web site: http://www.civilwarnews.com

The Civil War Preservation Trust
1331 H Street NW, Suite 1001
Washington, DC 20005
(202) 367-1861
Web site: http://www.civilwar.org

Military Intelligence Corps Association
P.O. Box 13020
Fort Huachuca, AZ 85670
(520) 459-7745
Web site: http://www.micorps.org

The National Civil War Museum
One Lincoln Circle at Reservoir Park
P.O. Box 1861
Harrisburg, PA 17105-1861
(717) 260-1861
Web site: http://nationalcivilwarmuseum.org

U.S. Army Women's Museum
2100 Adams Avenue
Building P-5219
Fort Lee, VA 23801-2100
(804) 734-4326
Web site: http://www.awm.lee.army.mil

Washington Civil War Association
P.O. Box 3043
Arlington, WA 98223
(800) 260-5997
Web site: http://www.wcwa.net

WEB SITES
Due to the changing nature of Internet links, the Rosen Publishing Group, Inc., has developed an online list of Web sites related to the subject of this book. This site is updated regularly. Please use this link to access the list:

http://www.rosenlinks.com/aww/unio

For Further Reading

Bakeless, John. *Spies of the Confederacy.* Mineola, NY: Dover Publications, 1997.

Boyd, Belle. *Belle Boyd in Camp and Prison.* Baton Rouge, LA: Louisiana State University Press, 1998.

Brooks, Victor. *Spies in the Civil War* (Untold History of the Civil War). Broomall, PA: Chelsea House, 1999.

Caravantes, Peggy. *Petticoat Spies: Six Women Spies of the Civil War.* Greensboro, NC: Morgan Reynolds, 2002.

Chang, Ina. *A Separate Battle: Women and the Civil War.* New York: Puffin, 1996.

Currie, Stephen. *Women of the Civil War.* San Diego: Lucent Books, 2002.

Fishel, Edwin C. *The Secret War for the Union: The Untold Story of Military Intelligence in the Civil War.* Boston: Houghton Mifflin Company, 1998.

Jones, Wilmer L. *Behind Enemy Lines: Civil War Spies, Raiders, and Guerrillas.* Navasota, TX: Taylor Publications, 2001.

Markle, Donald E. *Spies and Spymasters of the Civil War.* New York: Hippocrene Books, 1999.

Stern, Philip Van Doren. *Secret Missions of the Civil War: First-hand Accounts by Men and Women Who Risked Their Lives in Underground Activities for the North and the South.* Walnut Creek, CA: Bonanza Books, 1990.

Wakeman, Sarah Rosetta. *An Uncommon Soldier: The Civil War Letters of Sarah Rosetta Wakeman.* Edited by Lauren Cook Burgess. New York: Oxford University Press, 1996.

Bibliography

Axelrod, Alan. *The War Between the Spies: A History of Espionage During the American Civil War.* Boston: Atlantic Monthly Press, 1992.

Blanton, Deanne, and Lauren M. Cook. *They Fought Like Demons: Women Soldiers in the American Civil War.* Baton Rouge, LA: Louisiana State University Press, 2002.

Bradford, Sarah. *Harriet Tubman: The Moses of Her People.* Bedford, MA: Applewood Books, 1886.

Dannet, Sylvia G. *She Rode with the Generals: The True and Incredible Story of Sarah Emma Seelye, Alias Franklin Thompson.* New York: Thomas Nelson and Sons, 1960.

Eggleston, Larry G. *Women in the Civil War: Extraordinary Stories of Soldiers, Spies, Nurses, Doctors, Crusaders, and Others.* Jefferson, NC: McFarland & Company, 2003.

Leonard, Elizabeth, D. *Yankee Women: Gender Battles in the Civil War.* New York: W. W. Norton & Company, 1994.

Massey, Mary Elizabeth. *Women in the Civil War.* Lincoln, NE: University of Nebraska Press, 1994.

Petry, Ann. *Harriet Tubman: Conductor on the Underground Railroad.* New York: Harper Trophy, 1996.

Van Lew, Elizabeth L., and David D. Ryan, ed. *A Yankee Spy in Richmond: The Civil War Diary of "Crazy Bet" Van Lew.* Mechanicsburg, PA: Stackpole Books, 1996.

Source Notes

Chapter One

1. Laura Micham, "Sarah E. Thompson Papers, 1859–1898," Duke University. Retrieved May 20, 2003 (http://scriptorium.lib.duke.edu/thompson).
2. Ibid.
3. David Ray Skinner, "John Hunt Morgan: A Southern Legend," Historic Harrison County Web Site. Retrieved April 26, 2003 (http://historic.shcsc.k12.in.us/civilwar/gjhm.htm).
4. Ibid.
5. Micham.
6. Larry G. Eggleston, *Women in the Civil War: Extraordinary Stories of Soldiers, Spies, Nurses, Doctors, Crusaders, and Others* (Jefferson, NC: McFarland & Company, 2003), p. 162.
7. Micham.
8. Sarah Thompson, "Letter to Honorable John Sherman from Sarah Thompson: April 19, 1879," Duke University. Retrieved April 16, 2003 (http//scriptorium.lib.duke.edu/thompson/1879-04-19/1879-04-19.html).

Chapter Two

1. Larry G. Eggleston, *Women in the Civil War: Extraordinary Stories of Soldiers, Spies, Nurses,*

Doctors, Crusaders, and Others (Jefferson, NC: McFarland & Company, 2003), p. 80.

2. Alan Axelrod, *The War Between the Spies: A History of Espionage During the American Civil War* (Boston: Atlantic Monthly Press, 1992), p. 104.

3. Elizabeth L. Van Lew, *A Yankee Spy in Richmond: The Civil War Diary of "Crazy Bet" Van Lew*, edited by David D. Ryan (Mechanicsburg, PA: Stackpole Books, 1996), p. 27.

4. Harnett T. Kane, "Spies for the Blue and Gray." Retrieved April 3, 2003 (http//www. civilwarhome.com/crazybet.htm).

5. Van Lew, p. 8.

6. Ibid., p. 11.

7. Eggleston, p. 82.

8. Ibid., p. 82.

9. Ibid., p. 83.

10. Ibid., p. 84.

Chapter Three

1. Mike Kendra, "Women in the Civil War: Mary Elizabeth Bowser," CivilWarTalk.com. Retrieved April 26, 2003 (http://www.kinkade.ws/ cwt_alt/resources/women/m_bowser.htm).

2. Elizabeth L. Van Lew, *A Yankee Spy in Richmond: The Civil War Diary of "Crazy Bet" Van Lew*, edited by David D. Ryan (Mechanicsburg, PA: Stackpole Books, 1996), p. 11.

3. Ibid., p. 11.

4. Ibid., p. 12.

5. Vertamae Grosvenor, "The Spy Who Served Me," NPR. Retrieved March 20, 2003 (http://www.npr.org/programs/morning/features/2002/apr/served/).
6. Ibid.
7. "Black History Profiles: Mary Elizabeth Bowser," *Richmond Times Dispatch*. Retrieved June 7, 2003 (http://www.timesdispatch.com/blackhistory/MGBQM54OAIC.html).
8. Ibid.

Chapter Four

1. Ann Petry, *Harriet Tubman: Conductor on the Underground Railroad* (New York: Harper Trophy, 1996), p. 31.
2. Sarah Bradford, *Harriet Tubman: The Moses of Her People* (Bedford, MA: Applewood Books, 1886), p. 100.
3. Lewis, Jone Johnson, "Harriet Tubman—Moses of Her People," *Women's History Guide*. Retrieved March 29, 2003 (http://www.womenshistory.about.com).

Chapter Five

1. Carolyn Swift, "Cushman, Civil War Spy, Is a SLV Legend," *Santa Cruz Sentinel* (Santa Cruz, CA), March 12, 2000.
2. Larry G. Eggleston, *Women in the Civil War: Extraordinary Stories of Soldiers, Spies, Nurses, Doctors, Crusaders, and Others* (Jefferson, NC: McFarland & Company, 2003), p. 126.

3. Swift.
4. Eggleston, p. 127.
5. Mary Elizabeth Massey, *Women in the Civil War* (Lincoln, NE: University of Nebraska Press, 1966), p. 102.

Chapter Six

1. Sarah Emma Edmonds, *Nurse and Spy in the Union Army* (Scituate, MA: Digital Scanning, 2000), p. 218.
2. Sylvia G. Dannet, *She Rode with the Generals: The True and Incredible Story of Sarah Emma Seelye, Alias Franklin Thompson* (New York: Thomas Nelson and Sons, 1960), pp. 24–25.
3. Ibid., p. 27.
4. Edmonds, p. 163.
5. Dannet, p. 224.
6. Ibid., p. 275.

Chapter Seven

1. Elaine Schneider, "Civil War Heroines: Information on Sojourner Truth, Rebecca Wright and Mary Todd Lincoln." Retrieved May 12, 2003 (http://nv.essortment.com/herionessojourn_rjek.htm).
2. Mary Elizabeth Massey, *Women in the Civil War* (Lincoln, NE: University of Nebraska Press, 1966), p. 104.
3. Larry G. Eggleston, *Women in the Civil War: Extraordinary Stories of Soldiers, Spies, Nurses,*

Doctors, Crusaders, and Others (Jefferson, NC: McFarland and Company, 2003), p. 180.

4. Elizabeth D. Leonard, *Yankee Women: Gender Battles in the Civil War* (New York: W. W. Norton & Company, 1994), p. 136.

5. Ibid., p. 138.

6. Ibid., p. 139.

Index

About the Author

Lois Sakany is a freelance writer who lives in Brooklyn, New York.

Photo Credits

Cover © Bettmann/Corbis; p. 5 Civil War Treasures from the New-York Historical Society; p. 6 © Hulton Archive/Getty Images; pp. 8, 15, 25, 37, 41, 43, 48, 64, 74, 76, 86, 91 Prints and Photographs Division, Library of Congress; pp. 12, 14 © Corbis; pp. 17, 21 Rare Book, Manuscript and Special Collections Library, Duke University; p. 24 Virginia Historical Society; pp. 28, 32 Civil War Photograph Collection, Library of Congress; p. 39 Ohio Historical Center Archives Library; pp. 52, 55, 56 © AP/Wide World Photos; pp. 59, 66, 70, 79, 82 The New York Public Library; p. 61 The National Portrait Gallery, Smithsonian Institution/Art Resource, NY; p. 73 courtesy of State Archives of Michigan, Lansing, MI; p. 88 National Museum of Health and Medicine, Washington, DC.

Designer: Evelyn Horovicz; **Editor:** Joann Jovinelly; **Photo Researcher:** Adriana Skura